Sabine Lohf

Nature Crafts

Outdoor magic using
natural materials
for creative crafts

CP CHILDRENS PRESS®
CHICAGO

14669

745
L

Thanks to Maja, Lea, Inka, Jule, and
Angela, who all helped me with this book.

Translation by Mrs. Werner Lippmann and Mrs. Ruth Bookey

Library of Congress Cataloging-in-Publication Data

Lohf, Sabine.
    [Komm, wir verzaubern den Wald.   English]
    Nature crafts / Sabine Lohf.
        p. cm.
    Summary: Describes a variety of craft projects using flowers,
shells, leaves, vegetables, and other materials found in nature.
    ISBN 0-516-09257-X
    1. Nature craft—Juvenile literature.   [1. Nature craft.
2. Handicraft.] I. Title.
TT157.L563 1990
745.5—dc20

89-49552
CIP
AC

Published in the United States in 1990 by Childrens Press®, Inc.,
5440 North Cumberland Avenue, Chicago, IL 60656.

Sabine Lohf

Nature Crafts

Contents

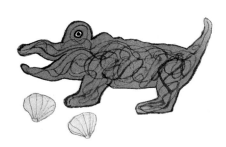

Outdoor Magic

When you are in the woods, in a meadow, or beside a brook, take a very close look. You will discover all sorts of interesting things: wild animals, a flower princess, a small bark sailor. You may not recognize them right away, so you will have to help make them more recognizable by using string, clay, scissors, needles, toothpicks, and colored paper, as well as natural materials you find outdoors.

In this book we will show you some of the outdoor magic we created. We discovered many new things we could use for our outdoor magic, and you will too. Come on, let's get started!

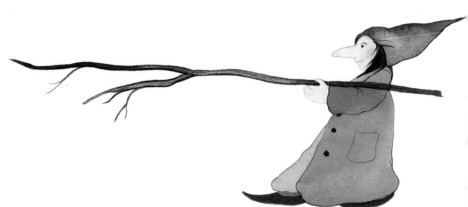

By the Pond

Julie, Jane, and Lee set a few votive candles on pieces of bark. They float the bark on the pond. Years ago people used to float candles to celebrate the end of winter and the lengthening of the days. As it gets dark outside, you can see the reflection of the candles floating on the pond.

In the Meadow

When you see the meadow glowing with yellow dandelions, you know that many other flowers will be blooming soon. Julie will show Jane and Lee how to make a flower wreath to wear like a crown.

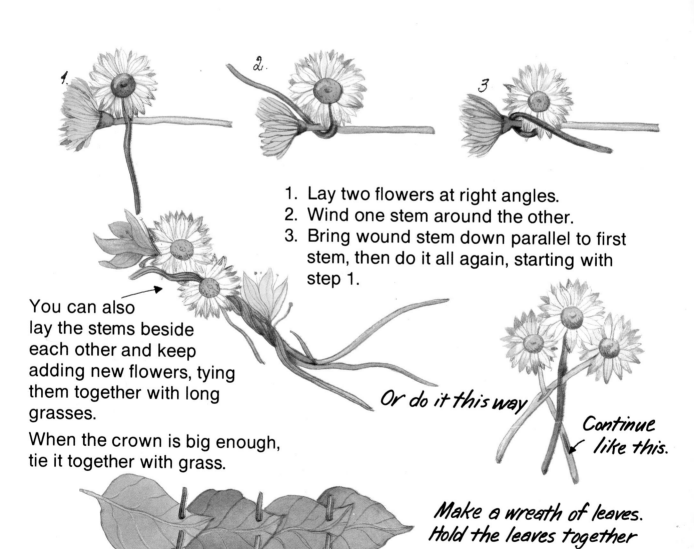

1. Lay two flowers at right angles.
2. Wind one stem around the other.
3. Bring wound stem down parallel to first stem, then do it all again, starting with step 1.

You can also lay the stems beside each other and keep adding new flowers, tying them together with long grasses.

When the crown is big enough, tie it together with grass.

Or do it this way

Continue like this.

Make a wreath of leaves. Hold the leaves together with small sticks.

The girls hung their first wreath on a post so that everyone could see how pretty it looked. Looking at the wreath might give you new and even better ideas about how to make such a wreath or crown.

Dandelion top

Use 2 petals as arms. Tie the ends with thread.

Stick the body onto a toothpick.

Tie a flower around the stem as a crown.

Leaf crown

The flowers look as soft as silk. Lee holds a flower by its stem. Julie and Jane wind a thread around some of the petals. Soon the girls make a whole flower family and celebrate by having a party for the family and the Flower Princess. They serve berries on leaf plates.

On their way home, the girls discover some long grass. They use string to tie up and shape the grass into two Indians. They put them on two sticks and plant them beside the path. Now everyone who walks by can see these little grass Indians beside the path.

At the Brook

At the brook Julie, Jane, and Lee have already discovered how well wood floats. Many small pieces of bark look like small boats, and with a toothpick mast and a leaf sail you can make little sailboats. Lee made a little sailor out of a piece of wood. He will sail down the brook. Jane collects small sticks to make a raft.

Tie the ends well.

To make a raft, tie several sticks together.

Make a sail out of cloth and tie it onto a stick.

Fasten the mast to the center of the raft.

12

The raft floats fast down the brook. The girls follow the raft for a while. Suddenly Lee yells, "Look, a little village with stick people just like our sailor!" Carl and Jack are hiding. They are pleased that someone has discovered their little village. Carl and Jack live near the brook. They brought glue and cardboard, string and scissors from home. This is the way they made the huts: Jack rolled a piece of cardboard and glued the ends together. Then he cut out a door. Carl and Jack glued sticks all around the cardboard. They had so much fun that they built another one, then a ladder and a raft. The village people are made from sticks with leaf clothes and painted faces. The boys and girls admired each other's creations and played beside the brook for a long time.

On the Beach

Fred and Lisa met while they were vacationing at the beach, and they often play together. One day the tide brought in a branch of a birch tree. With a tissue and a stick, they turned the branch into a sailboat. Fred drew and cut out some people for the boat. Of course these people needed a home, so Lisa and Fred built a sand castle.

the first monster

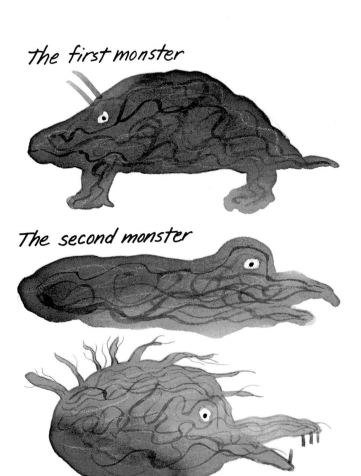

The second monster

The third monster

Will the sand castle be safe at night? Maybe someone will wreck the castle or steal the boat. Lisa has an idea: How about using some of the seaweed on the beach to make a monster to guard the castle? Lisa makes several different wild animals and decides that the crocodile would be the best guard.

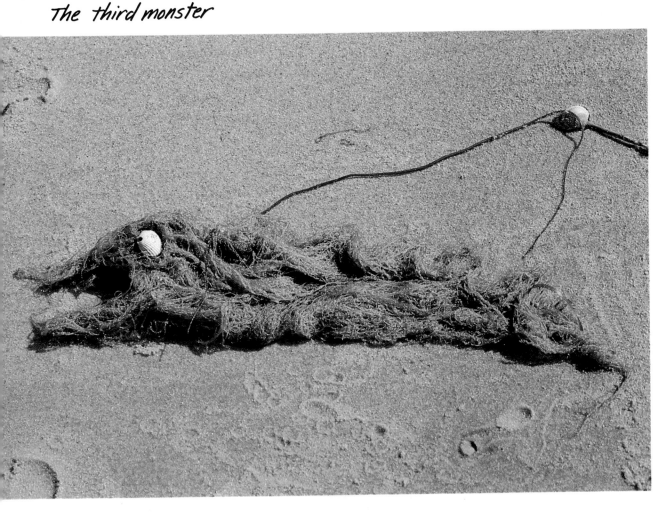

The crocodile needs a caretaker. So Fred uses some shells to make a man who holds the crocodile on a leash. The next day Lisa and Fred make a game for their yellow ball. They make a circular playing field with a hole in the very center, surrounded by two circular ditches. They will toss the ball at the playing field. They make up some rules: If the ball lands in the exact middle, the player scores 50 points. If it lands in the inner ditch, it's worth 30 points. The score for the outer ditch is 10 points. Fred and Lisa draw a crowd of children to their game.

Finish the face

Draw a large face without eyes in the sand. Each player takes two pebbles and tries to toss them into the face to make eyes.

Who'll hit the bull's-eye first?

Draw a target with a bull's-eye. Each player tries to hit the bull's-eye with a pebble.

Draw a monster

It's easy to draw in wet sand with a stick. Draw a sea monster. Be creative!

In the Forest

With a basket of clay, string, and scissors, Lee and Julie make some creature magic in the forest. Julie almost trips on a tree root that looks like a crocodile. With a mouth of pink clay and eyes of blue clay, the crocodile becomes quite recognizable. Jane finds a panther-shaped log. The girls find two branches that look like arms. Lee stands behind a tree and starts moving the branches as if they were alive. Julie notices another tree that looks as if it has big eyes. The girls tell their friends that there are wild animals in the forest.

Lee says that the forest is full of wild animals. She sees a wild pig between two roots. The girls notice a friendly little spider hiding in a bush. Later they meet a swan, another crocodile, a fish, and the Big Bad Wolf.

Hidden deep in the forest is a tree-stump castle. It looks totally isolated. Lee pushes some sticks into apples and says, "Later we can eat the apples, but first I'll make a king and queen for this abandoned castle!"

The King and Queen get crowns made from flowers that the girls have found along the path. The clothes are simply leaves wrapped around the sticks and fastened with thread.

The castle needs flags to show that the King is in residence. Under the shrubbery, Julie discovers a root that looks like a dog. She gives him a red paper tongue and wild eyes made of clay. He looks dangerous. The girls hide behind a big tree and hope someone will come by to see their creations. A mother and child walk by.

"Mommy, look! A castle with a king and queen!"

"That's impossible," says the mother. But then the mother looks closely. She is as delighted as the child.

Use clay to make eyes and a mouth.

Don't forget a crown made from a flower.

Tie on leaves with thread.

24

By the Roadside

Often you'll find beautiful big leaves growing at the side of the road. Tina and Sandy wanted to put a leaf-face on the road. They looked for little sticks for the nose and the mouth. They made many leaf pictures: a little man, a dog, a leaf-bird.

Lee discovered a leaf that looked like a pirate hat. She showed it to the others. Jane and Julie liked the pirate hat. The girls made marionettes from horse-chestnut leaves. How they made the marionettes is shown on the next page.

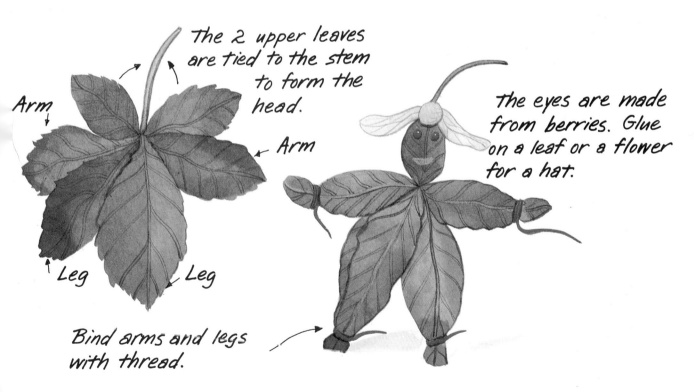

The 2 upper leaves
are tied to the stem
to form the
head.

Arm

Arm

Leg   Leg

Bind arms and legs
with thread.

The eyes are made
from berries. Glue
on a leaf or a flower
for a hat.

could you make marionettes
other kinds of leaves?

This is a pet hedgehog
that belongs to the
leaf man.

On the way home, Julie, Jane, and Lee found a pile of sticks. They had leftover string, so they made a real marionette. They call the marionette Fred Funny Legs. It looks funny when it dances. It makes them laugh.

Hold on here to move marionette.

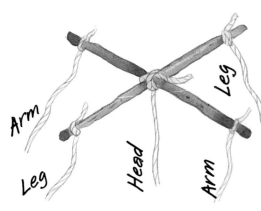

Arm

Leg

Head

Arm

Leg

1. Tie 2 sticks together crosswise.

2. Tie a long string on the end of each stick.

3. Tie the strings like this to the marionette.

Jane found a little stick with a nose. It looked as if it could dance. She colored the nose red with a crayon. Julie tied a feather dress on the stick to make a feather woman. Lee put a snail shell on a forked stick to make a snail man. They put the figures into the brook and watched them for a long time. Lee made up a story: Once upon a time there was a snail man and a feather woman. They looked so different from everyone else that nobody wanted them around. They walked in the woods for years. They slept on a moss bed or under a tree root. The feather woman was quite tired from all this walking and longed for a home. Julie said, "We will build a home for them tomorrow. I know already how we will do it!" Can you build them a home?

Use berries or little stones for eyes.

Fasten the little apple people together with toothpicks.

For a nose, fasten a berry with a pin.

In the Orchard

Julie and Lee are supposed to gather fallen apples for applesauce. But that can wait. Lee would rather make little appl people. She collects apples, leaves, and little sticks. She makes one little apple person after another. It is a funny little group. Jane is very enthusiastic when she sees them. She sees many more fallen apples at the other end of the orchard. The gir take them home and make even more little apple people. The girl wonder how it would be if the re apple people met the green app people in the orchard one evening!

In the Fields

Carl and Jack found many leftover potatoes on a harvested field. They made potato people with toothpicks and little sticks. The potato figures came out so well that Jack said enthusiastically, "We will have a party in honor of the Potato King!"

They took many potatoes home in a bag and made all kinds of funny animals like the ones below.

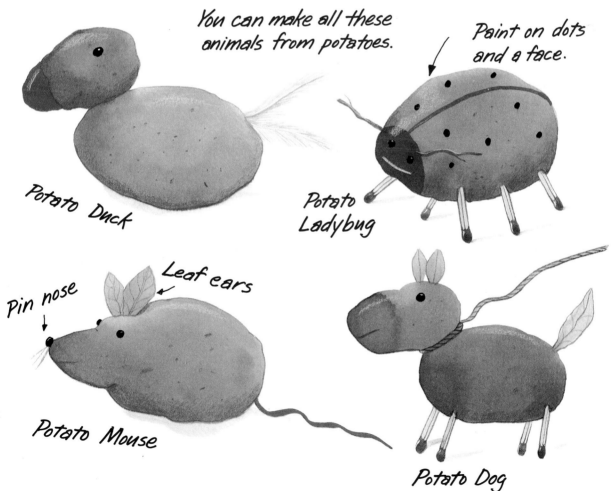

You can make all these animals from potatoes.

Potato Duck

Paint on dots and a face.

Potato Ladybug

Pin nose

Leaf ears

Potato Mouse

Potato Dog

33

When Julie, Lee, and Jane walk by a cornfield, they see that the farmer is harvesting corn with a big machine. They ask him what he will do with the corn. He gives them a few ears when they leave. A corn ear has many green leaves outside. Jane bends back a few leaves and sees something like long blond hair (the silk). The girls get an idea: They will make two royal corn couples, one yellow and one green. Julie likes the green pair better because it looks so mysterious. Lee likes the yellow pair better. Jane thinks both are beautiful. And here is how they made them!

All the leaves are opened up for this little corn person.

On top of the head, bind up a few leaves with a thin thread.

Scratch in the face with a needle.

Press the stem into the ground.

This corn is standing upside down.

In the Park

Jack and Carl were in the park. They filled a big basket with nuts, feathers, acorns, and rose hips to take home. They got together to build something with Julie, Jane, Lee, and their parents, who wanted to help too. Everyone had a different idea. Carl's father made a little horse-chestnut basket, the way he had made them when he was a child. They also made a hedgehog, a rose-hip woman, an owl, a nut cat, a wide-mouthed frog, and many more things.

Soft, beautiful moss grows under some trees.
Lee says, "If I were a forest dwarf, I would live in
a moss house." Julie suggests that they build a
moss house for the many rose-hip dwarfs. You
cannot see the dwarfs because they work in a
cave and only come out at night to go home.
Jane and Lee build a scaffolding of twigs. They
cover it all with moss and talk very quietly
together so that they won't frighten the dwarfs!

See, here come the dwarfs out of the cave! They wear leaf clothes, and some carry flower umbrellas. They are waiting under the mushroom for the others so that they can all go home together! They put the rose-hip dwarf children to bed. Then they wrap themselves in an oak-leaf sleeping bag and dream.

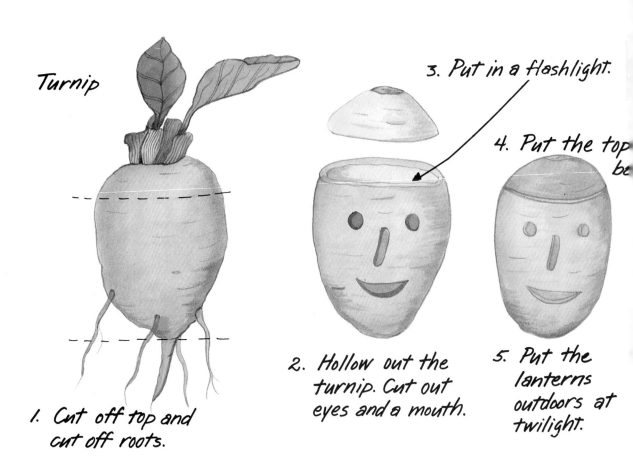

Turnip

1. Cut off top and cut off roots.

2. Hollow out the turnip. Cut out eyes and a mouth.

3. Put in a flashlight.

4. Put the top be

5. Put the lanterns outdoors at twilight.

In the Front Yard

Lee's mother bought two big turnips at the store. The girls decided to make turnip ghost lanterns with them. Since they have only two turnips, Jane, the third girl, will carve a melon instead. They all hollow out their vegetables. The melon is easier to cut! Then the girls put small flashlights inside the hollowed-out vegetables. They put their new lanterns in front of the house, where they glow like ugly ghosts!

In the winter, snow monsters lurk all over the yard! They are even on the branches. They rest lazily on dry grass. You have to look closely to discover them all. The icicles hanging from the roof look like the whiskers of a walrus. If you stick lots of icicles into the ground, you can make an ice palace for an ice queen!

If the snow king looks like this photo, he will certainly have to have a crown. But maybe he is only a simple snowman after all. You rarely see a real snow king.

Jane has made two snowmen in her yard, one small and one large. The big one looks very happy with Lee's cap, even if his ears have to stay cold. Julie can think of many more things to make out of snow. It is to late to get it all done today, but tomorrow they will continue!

INDEX